BOOK ANALYSIS

Written by Danny Dejonghe
Translated by Emma Lunt

AF131403

Blindness

BY JOSÉ SARAMAGO

JOSÉ SARAMAGO

PORTUGUESE WRITER AND JOURNALIST

- **Born in Azinhaga, Portugal in 1922**
- **Died in Lanzarote (Canary Islands, Spain) in 2010**
- **Notable works:**
  - *The Gospel According to Jesus Christ* (1991), novel
  - *The Double* (2002), novel
  - *Seeing* (2004), novel

José Saramago was born in Portugal in 1922 to a humble family. At the age of 12, he was forced to drop out of school to train as a locksmith. He tried his hand at various jobs, working as a journalist for *Diário de Notícias*, then as a translator before beginning a career in literature. His first novel, *Terra do Pecado* (*Land of Sin*), was published in 1947, but it was not until the publication of his first translated work in 1982, *Baltasar and Blimunda,* that he became recognised for his work.

Saramago was a member of the Communist party and fled to the Canary Islands in 1991 when his work *The Gospel According to Jesus Christ* was judged as blasphemous and censored in his country. Having received honorary doctorates from numerous French universities, he then received the Camões prize in 1995; the most prestigious prize for literature in Portugal. Three years later, he won the Nobel Prize for literature. His works, which include novels, essays, poetry and plays, have been translated into numerous languages and published throughout the world.

BLINDNESS

THE DECLINE OF SOCIETY THROUGH THE METAPHOR OF BLINDNESS

- **Genre:** novel
- **Reference edition:** Saramago, J. (2013) *Blindness*. Trans. Pontiero, G. London: Vintage Books.
- **First edition:** 1995
- **Themes:** blindness, confinement, apocalyptic world, rebellion, insanity, hope, violence, dictatorship, anarchy, dehumanisation, barbarism, survival

Blindness, originally published in Portugal in 1995, was translated into English three years later and published by Harcourt. It all begins in a cosmopolitan and crowded, yet unnamed, city. At a set of traffic lights, a car comes to a stop and the driver suddenly goes blind. This is followed by a series of similar phenomena.

The people affected by this blindness epidemic are quarantined in an asylum with deplorable living conditions in which society has become dehumanised. Despite this sombre atmosphere, there is still a ray of hope: somebody has been spared from the contagion. It is the ophthalmologist's wife, who will guide the blind back towards civilisation.

SUMMARY

A BLINDNESS EPIDEMIC

In an unnamed city, a driver has stopped at a crossroads when he suddenly loses his sight. A young man offers to drive him home, but takes advantage of him and steals his car. This young man then becomes blind himself. The first blind man goes to see an ophthalmologist, accompanied by his wife. There are several people in the waiting room: a beautiful young woman who wears tinted glasses to hide her conjunctivitis, a boy with a squint and an old man who needs an operation on his cataract and wears an eyepatch. The doctor is perplexed by the man's illness; he observes that the patient is blind but the eye is undamaged. That night, while researching this 'illness', the doctor loses his sight.

The authorities, warned of this phenomenon, put all the contagious blind people in quarantine in an asylum. Among them are the original blind man, the car thief, the young woman with conjunctivitis and the squinting child. The ophthalmologist and his wife are also there, although the latter is only pretending to be blind in order to stay with her husband. Later on the old man with the eyepatch, the first blind man's wife and the secretary from the ophthalmologist's office arrive. The sufferers decide to call the illness the white evil, as all they see is white.

DEHUMANISED SOCIETY

The conditions in the insane asylum are almost inhumane and bear a strong resemblance to those of Nazi concentration camps. The patients receive little food or care, the building is dirty and always full of new patients who arrive every day in their dozens, and everybody is watched by guards who are ready to shoot anyone who may attempt to escape. It is the young car thief who suffers this fate when he tries to flee, despite an injury on his thigh inflicted by the young woman after he made an inappropriate gesture.

Despite her many efforts to be contaminated, the doctor's wife resists the epidemic but, nevertheless, continues to fake blindness in order to avoid being excluded. The fact that she can still see allows her to find her way around and to help the blind with various daily tasks, becoming a sort of guide for them.

Due to the high influx of patients, the authorities decide to eradicate the illness through "wholesale liquidation" (p. 81) and so several patients are shot by the guards. In response, the blind people decide to unite and support each other. But this unison does not last long and gives way to self-interest: arguments break out notably during the division of food, as everybody wants more than their fair share, or when the racket that some people make disturbs others' sleep. The micro-society that develops places individual needs over collective needs. The situation worsens with the arrival of the last blind people, the majority of whom are thugs who ration the food and force the others to pay them; if anyone refuses, they are beaten.

THE VIOLENCE INCREASES

Soon, the latest arrivals establish a dictatorship and as the days pass, the horror intensifies. Although at first the blind crooks had limited themselves to simply rationing food, now, due to their strong sexual appetite, they demand women, whom they rape, in return for food. While some of the women decide to rebel, a group of seven women, including the ophthalmologist's wife and the woman with the dark glasses, decide to give themselves to the barbaric group so that they can continue to eat. They are savagely raped, with one woman dying from her injuries. The sexual extortion continues and the doctor's wife ends up killing the leader of the crooks.

Far from mollifying the situation, the deceased leader is quickly replaced by another, an accountant who, until then, had been harmless. He decides to deprive the other inmates of all food, while the authorities have decided to no longer deliver supplies to them. Some people, including the ophthalmologist and his wife, the first blind man and his wife, the young boy, the young woman with conjunctivitis and the old man with the eyepatch come up with a plan to steal food from the crooks.

A short while later, the group of inmates decide to rebel by any means possible, leading to an epic battle. However, it ends in defeat. Finally, an unknown woman sets fire to the building, defeating the crooks and destroying the asylum at the same time. Everybody is free to go into the city once again.

THE BLIND IN THE CITY

Upon leaving the asylum, the blind people feel disorientated and scared as they rediscover the environment around them. They realise that everybody in the city has gone blind, meaning that it's every man for himself when it comes to food and drink. After finding shelter for the group, the ophthalmologist's wife decides to go in search of supplies and finds a basement full of them, which is inaccessible for the blind people. She returns to her friends in the shelter and feeds them.

Having regained their strength, they decide to look for each person's house. The first home they visit is that of the young woman with the dark glasses who hopes to find her parents. Unfortunately, they have disappeared. The next morning, they return to the city and arrive in the area where the doctor and his wife live. In their apartment, the group rediscover the taste of water and the joy of being able to wash. After spending the night there, the ophthalmologist's wife decides to leave again in search of food. The first blind man and his wife go with her, hoping to return to their house. But they discover that a writer and his family have taken over. The couple, who now live with the group, decide to allow the writer to stay there, as private property is one of many concepts forgotten by the population since the blindness epidemic.

SIGHT RETURNS

The next day, during another expedition to find food, the ophthalmologist and his wife observe that the city is going from bad to worse:

> "The state of the streets got worse with every passing hour. The rubbish seemed to increase during the hours of darkness, it was as if from outside, from some unknown country where they still had a normal life, they were coming in the night to empty their dustbins..." (p. 293).

When they arrive at the store, the woman discovers dozens of bodies on the stairs leading to the hideaway. Shocked by what she sees, she collapses. With her husband's help, she manages to make her way into a religious temple where the couple make another alarming discovery: all the religious figures (Jesus, Mary, the saints, etc.) are blindfolded.

They return to the apartment after a frugal meal. That night a miracle occurs: the first blind man regains his sight as suddenly as he lost it. The same thing quickly happens for each member of the group as well as the rest of the city. The reason for this sudden blindness and recovery forever remains a mystery.

CHARACTER STUDY

The first blind man suddenly loses his sight while stopped at a red light. Somebody comes to help him but takes advantage of the situation and steals his car. From then on, the first blind man holds a grudge against the thief.

This character does not have a central role; he features mainly when he leads the expeditions into the other asylum dormitories or when he has to help his group find food. He loves his wife very much and is never separated from her. He is also very possessive towards her: when she decides to give herself to the crooks, he orders her not to go. He is also the first to recover his sight.

THE CAR THIEF

This young man volunteers to take the first blind man home, but takes advantage of the situation by stealing his car. In turn, he loses his own sight and is quarantined with the others in the asylum.

Inside the community he acts inappropriately, particularly with the women. One of the women defends herself and seriously injures his leg. When he can no longer put up with imprisonment, he tries to escape, but is killed by the guards who watch the building before he reaches the exit.

THE YOUNG WOMAN WITH DARK GLASSES

This young woman goes to see the ophthalmologist for conjunctivitis; a few hours later she loses her sight.

She seems to like male contact but never allows herself to be pushed around when she is annoyed and proves herself to be a strong character. She is also protective and maternal with both the young boy with a squint and the ophthalmologist's wife when she finds her on the verge of a nervous breakdown.

On returning to the city, she leaves to find her apartment which she shared which her parents but finds nobody there. At the end of the book, she wants to live with the old man with the eyepatch, with whom she had shared an embrace one night but claims not to be in love with him. She is the second person to finally regain her vision.

THE OLD MAN WITH THE EYEPATCH

This old man is another one of the ophthalmologist's patients who went blind. When he arrives at the asylum, all he brings is a radio so that he and his companions can stay up to date with what is happening outside. When the crooks arrive he is more discrete, not wanting to have the only thing he owns stolen. From then on, he listens to the news alone, hidden under his bedcovers, before giving the others a summary of what he has heard.

At the end of the novel, he confesses that he wants to live with the young woman with dark glasses.

THE OPHTHALMOLOGIST

The doctor had consultations with four of the blind people before being struck with the blindness himself. Despite his research, he is unable to explain the origin of the illness. When he loses his sight, he is shut in the asylum with his wife where he is designated 'leader of the barracks'. Throughout the story, he represents the voice of reason.

He is also a strong source of support for his wife who is pretending to be blind. While the others only perceive the horror using their other senses, she is aware of everything that is happening and almost has a nervous breakdown on multiple occasions.

He is the third person to regain his sight at the end of the book.

THE OPHTHALMOLOGIST'S WIFE

The ophthalmologist's wife is the only person in the story not to go blind and no physical or psychological explanation is given. This raises the question: "why her?" Without a doubt, part of the answer lies in the fact that she is a woman with strong morals: she is sensitive and generous, and she doesn't use her power to dominate, instead using it to help those close to her.

Furthermore, by pretending to be blind to accompany her husband to the asylum, she turns out to be an important help to the blind people. Whether she is taking them to the toilet, collecting their food, or even helping her husband bury the dead (a task which the inmates must undertake), she plays her role as a guide. She ensures that the group does not descend into complete depravity and helps them maintain some dignity.

She is usually a woman with nerves of steel but she begins to fall apart when the living conditions of the inmates become inhumane. It is also her who kills the leader of the crooks. When the asylum is set on fire and the group end up on the streets, she is in charge of rationing. It is thanks to her ability to see that she can immediately find what she is looking for. After spotting a staircase next to an out-of-service lift, she goes down it and discovers a room full of food.

Throughout the novel, she becomes aware of her role as protector and of the psychological changes that the newly-blind population have experienced. When everybody regains their sight, she is overwhelmed with joy knowing that her ordeal is finally over.

THE BAND OF BLIND CROOKS

The band of blind crooks arrives at the asylum shortly after the first protagonists. To some extent, they represent the powers found at the top of totalitarian societies, who expect more rights than others. It is also they who hold the inmates to ransom in order to get their food and they don't think twice about using armed force to get what they want. As well as stealing, they reduce the freedom that the others have, banning them from the toilets and raping the women. The author often uses animalistic vocabulary to describe their behaviour.

The whole group perishes in the fire at the asylum, started by an unknown woman.

The blind accountant

Within the blind crooks' ranks there is an accountant who reads and writes in braille. He seems to feel some regret towards the systems put in place by his group. While, at first, he doesn't seem to share their convictions, he stays with the group for the material comfort it brings him.

When the ophthalmologist's wife kills the leader of the crooks, the blind accountant decides to grab his gun and proclaims himself as leader. He becomes a much harsher leader than the previous one, going as far as depriving the other inmates of food. However, within his group he suffers from a cruel lack of authority:

> "After the tragic death of their first leader, all spirit of discipline or sense of obedience had gone in the ward, the serious error on the part of the blind accountant was to have thought that it was enough to take possession of the gun in order to usurp power, but the result was exactly the opposite, each time he fires, the shot backfires, in other words, with each shot fired, he loses a little more authority..." (p. 199).

He dies in the fire at the asylum along with the other blind crooks.

ANALYSIS

FANTASY IN THE NOVEL-ESSAY

José Saramago's work can be compared with a novel-essay. The similarities between his story and the essay genre are visible from the title. In fact, *Blindness* was originally titled *Ensaio sobre a Cegueira*, which can be translated as *"Essay on Blindness"*. He himself admits his love for this genre, as it allows him to overcome certain worries or obsessions.

In *Blindness*, the author uses a simple premise but adds an element of fantasy: if everybody lost their sight at the same time, how would society react? By removing one of our five senses, the author makes us question our human condition. We therefore think that everything we possess is ours. Yet reality is not so lenient and everything can topple from one day to the next. While blind, the characters seem to have completely lost their bearings and in the space of a few weeks, all society is in chaos.

Within *Blindness*, Saramago undertakes a literary, philosophical and sociological experiment by introducing a fantastical element into a real-life universe, before watching to see what happens.

A METAPHORICAL NOVEL

Blindness is Saramago's first metaphorical novel. This literary style uses strong imagery to give life to a concept, an abstract reality. A popular style in the Middle Ages – mainly thanks to *Le Roman de la Rose* (13th century) by Guillaume de Lorris (French poet, around 1200-around 1238) and Jean de Meung (French poet, around 1240-around 1305), where the rose represents a loved woman – it came back into fashion with the novel *The Plague* (1947) by Albert Camus (French writer, 1913-1960), in which the plague is generally seen to represent Nazism.

THE BLINDNESS EPIDEMIC: A METAPHOR, BUT FOR WHAT?

Regarding Saramago's novel, he seems unwilling to explain the hidden meaning behind the sudden blindness as, according to him, this "could make the reader better understand more things than cold, scientific descriptions would..."[1] (Amorim, 2010: 102). Furthermore, even if the mystery remains, we can imagine the authors intentions "to awaken consciousness by inviting the reader to reflect more deeply" (*ibid.*: 4). And this awakening of consciousness should be universal: it affects all of humanity through unidentified characters evolving in an undetermined time and space.

Like Camus in *The Plague,* the author wants to warn the reader: is the blindness that affects almost the entire population of a city not a metaphor of the ignorance and deception that have always, and continue to, drag humans down to the level of beasts? Does it embody selfishness, intolerance and the fact that when it comes to others, we

---

1. All quotes taken from this text have been translated by BrightSummaries.com

are in fact blind as to what is happening before our eyes? As Saramago does not give an explicit response, it is up to the reader to find their own.

A METAPHOR FOR CONCENTRATION CAMPS

While it is possible to see the blindness epidemic as a representation of the hardening of our society, a more explicit metaphor appears in the novel: that of concentration camps. By reading about the living conditions of the patients in the asylum, it is impossible not to think of the concentration camps used by the Nazis during the Second World War (1939-1945). There are numerous parallels:

- The blind people are segregated in different dormitories depending on the cause of their illness (whether they had it originally or were contaminated). This is similar to the way in which the Nazis separated the men and the women upon entry to the camps to then choose who was most suitable for working;
- Living conditions are particularly difficult. It is dirty and food is rationed and limited;
- The asylum is guarded by soldiers who are under the order to shoot anybody who tries to flee, as was the case during the Second World War;
- In the same way that the imprisoned Jews were exterminated in large groups in the Nazi camps, the authorities in *Blindness* decide to eliminate a large number of the contaminated people;
- Finally, the inmates of the asylum, like the victims of the camps, suffer from dehumanisation. Living conditions

are so bad that, little by little, they begin to lose what makes them human.

THE THEME OF DEHUMANISATION

Dehumanisation is a very present theme in Saramago's novel. While it begins with the atrocious conditions in the asylum, within a sort of psychological isolation, it continues after they leave the establishment: the streets of the city are full of chaos, horror, abject filth, and indignities to man (rubbish, excrement, cadavers, etc.).

> "He knew he was dirty, dirtier than he could ever remember having been in his life. There are many ways of becoming an animal, he thought, this is just the first of them." (p. 89)

Nevertheless, it is survival of the fittest and survival instincts that prevail.

Furthermore, while the fact that no character is given a name means that it is universal, it also reinforces the phenomenon of dehumanisation. The protagonists are only differentiated by their job (such as the ophthalmologist), their role in the plot (such as the first blind man) or by their physical characteristics (such as the old man with the eyepatch).

In the same way, perhaps the fact that it is the protagonists' sight that they lose, as opposed to any of the other senses, is a sign of a society that has taken a step back from culture – and therefore from its humanity. Indeed, aren't eyes necessary to access some forms of art, such as to admire a painting or marvel at a dance performance?

FURTHER REFLECTION

SOME QUESTIONS TO THINK ABOUT...

- *The Plague* by Albert Camus could be considered a metaphorical novel, like *Blindness*. Compare the two works.
- In this guide we have compared the conditions of detainment of the blind people with those of the Jews in the concentration camps. Compare the asylum in *Blindness* with the description of the concentration camps in *Le Mort qu'il faut* (2001) by Jorge Semprún and *If this is a Man* (1947) by Primo Levi.
- The novel presents various different societal models, both within the asylum and outside. Compare them; what differences and similarities can you notice?
- *Blindness* represents a society upturned by blindness and the necessary construction of a new society. Do you know any other novels that have the same premise?
- The reason as to why everybody regains their vision at the end of the novel remains a mystery. Construct a hypothesis to explain the sudden blindness and return of sight.
- If you were to suddenly go blind, like the characters in the novel, what sort of attitude would you adopt? Which category would you put yourself in?
- Do you know any of José Saramago's other novels? What are the similarities and differences between them and *Blindness*?
- In your opinion, why did the author choose to have the characters lose their sight? Would we reflect in the same way if the character had gone deaf?
- Try to create a character map for the novel: who are the

heroes? What would the protagonists be searching for? Etc.

- Comment on the following passage:

> "I don't think we did go blind, I think we are blind, Blind but seeing, Blind people who can see but do not see." (p. 309).

We want to hear from you!
Leave a comment on your online library
and share your favourite books on social media!

FURTHER READING

REFERENCE EDITION

- Saramago, J. (2013) *Blindness*. Trans. Pontiero, G. London: Vintage Books.

REFERENCE STUDIES

- Amorim S. (2010) *José Saramago. Art, théorie et éthique du roman*. Paris: L'Harmattan.
- Errera E. (2013) *José Saramago. Tous les discours de réception de prix Nobel de literature*. Paris: Flammarion, pp. 248-266.
- Fréjaville R. M. (2010) Les manifestations de l'horreur dans *Ensaio Sobre a Cegueira* de José Saramago. *Cahiers du CELEC*, issue 1. [Accessed 4 August 2016]. Available from:
<http://cahiersducelec.univ-st-etienne.fr/index.php?option=com_content&view=article&id=18%3Acahiers-du-celec-nd1&Itemid=2>

ADAPTATIONS

- *Blindness*. (2008) [Film] Fernando Meirelles. Dir. Japan, Brazil and Canada: Rhombus Media.

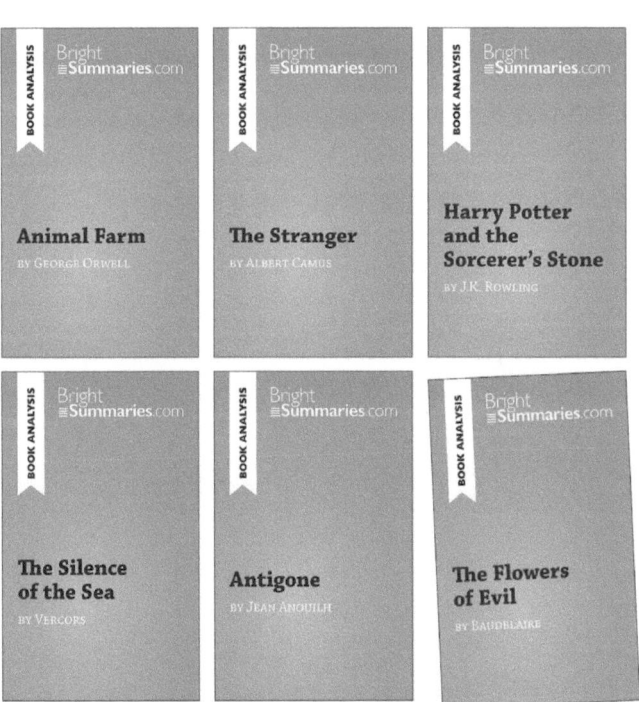